WEATHER

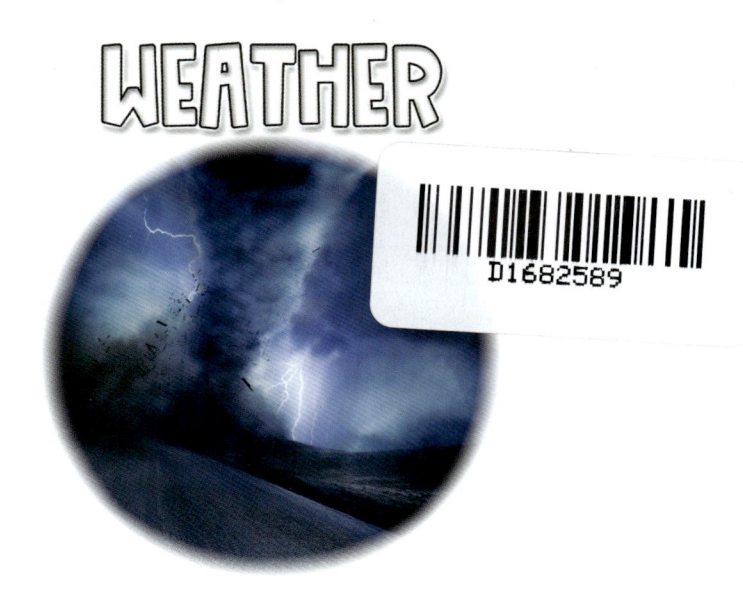

Written By: Anna DiGilio

All rights reserved. No part of this publication may be reproduced, distributed, or transmitted in any form or by any means, including photocopying, recording, or other electronic or mechanical methods, without the prior written permission of the publisher, except in the case of brief quotations embodied in critical reviews and certain other noncommercial uses permitted by copyright law.

For permission requests, write to the publisher:
Laprea Publishing
info@lapreapublishing.com

Website: www.GuidedReaders.com

ISBN: 978-1-64579-488-2

© 2019 Anna DiGilio
www.SimplySkilledTeaching.com

Printed in the United States of America

TABLE OF CONTENTS

Earth's Weather ....Page 4

Hot or Cold ....Page 5

Wind..Page 7

Clouds...Page 8

Rain and Snow ....Page 9

Storms...Page 10

Seasons...Page 11

Weather Tools ....Page 12

What Is the Weather Like?..............Page 14

Glossary..Page 15

Sunny day

Blizzard

Earth's Weather

There are many kinds of <u>weather</u>. Weather changes. It changes from day to day. It changes from month to month. It changes from year to year.

What is weather? Let's find out!

Tornado

Rainstorm

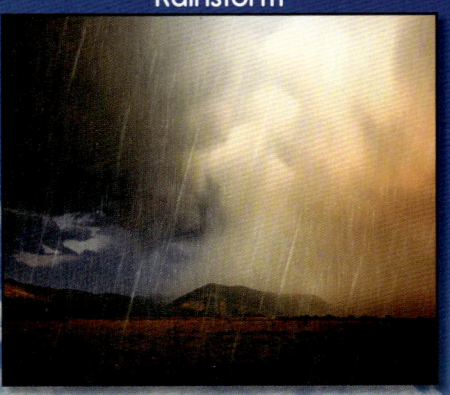

Hot

Warm

Hot or Cold

The weather can be hot. It can be warm. It can be cool. It can be cold.

Cool

Cold

It's warmer during the day.

It is daytime. The weather is warm. It is nighttime. The weather is cool.

It gets cooler at night.

Wind

Wind is moving air. Wind blows. Wind can be warm or cold. Wind can be gentle or strong.

Clouds

Some clouds are white. Some are gray. Some are thin. Some are like <u>blankets</u>.

Rain and Snow

Rain falls from clouds. Snow falls from clouds. Ice falls from clouds.

Rain

Ice

Snow

Storms

    <u>Storms</u> bring strong winds. Storms can bring rain. They can bring snow. They can bring <u>thunder</u> and <u>lightning</u>.

Spring

Summer

Seasons

The weather changes with the seasons. Spring is warm. Summer is hot. Fall is cool. Winter is cold. We wear different clothes in different season.

Fall

Winter

Weather Tools

<u>Tools</u> help us learn about the weather.

A *thermometer* tells us how hot or cold it is.

An *anemometer* tells us how fast the wind is blowing.

A *rain gauge* (GAYJ) tells us how much rain fell.

A *barometer* tells us if the weather will be sunny and dry or wet and stormy.

What Is the Weather Like?

What is the weather like now? How does it help you to know about the weather?

GLOSSARY

<u>blankets</u>
cloth coverings put on a bed to keep people warm

<u>lightning</u>
a flash of light in the sky during some storms

<u>storms</u>
events with strong winds and rain, thunder, lightning, or snow

<u>thunder</u>
a loud sound that follows lightning

GLOSSARY

<u>tools</u>
things held in the hand and used to do a job

<u>weather</u>
the state of the air at a certain time and place, such as hot, cold, clear, cloudy, or rainy